Campbell's

Quick&Easy
Recipes

pil

Publications International, Ltd.

Special thanks to the Campbell's Kitchen and Jane M. Freiman, Group Manager, and Catherine Marschean-Spivak, Group Manager.

Pictured on the front cover: Baked Pork Chops with Garden Stuffing *(page 36)*.

Pictured on the back cover (clockwise from top right): Saucy Mario Sandwiches *(page 9)*, Zucchini, Chicken & Rice Casserole *(page 56)*, Beef Taco Skillet *(page 49), and* Creamy 3-Cheese Pasta *(page 86)*.

ISBN-13: 978-1-60553-725-2
ISBN-10: 1-60553-725-X

Manufactured in China.

8 7 6 5 4 3 2 1

Microwave Cooking: Microwave ovens vary in wattage. Use the cooking times as guidelines and check for doneness before adding more time.

Preparation/Cooking Times: Preparation times are based on the approximate amount of time required to assemble the recipe before cooking, baking, chilling or serving. These times include preparation steps such as measuring, chopping and mixing. The fact that some preparations and cooking can be done simultaneously is taken into account. Preparation of optional ingredients and serving suggestions is not included.

Contents

30 Minutes to Dinner

From start to finish in half an hour or less

Shrimp & Corn Chowder with Sun-Dried Tomatoes

MAKES 4 SERVINGS ■ **PREP TIME:** 5 MINUTES ■ **COOK TIME:** 20 MINUTES

1. Heat the soup, half-and-half, corn and tomatoes in a 2-quart saucepan over medium heat to a boil. Cover and reduce the heat to low. Cook for 10 minutes.

2. Stir in the shrimp and chives and heat through.

3. Season to taste with black pepper.

■ Kitchen Tip

For a lighter version, substitute skim milk for the half-and-half.

 + + +

| 1 can (10¾ ounces) Campbell's® Condensed Cream of Potato Soup | 1½ cups half-and-half | 2 cups whole kernel corn, drained |

**2 tablespoons
sun-dried tomatoes,
cut in strips**

**1 cup small *or* medium
cooked shrimp**

**2 tablespoons chopped
fresh chives**

Chipotle Pork Taco Cups

MAKES 10 SERVINGS ■ **PREP TIME:** 15 MINUTES
BAKE TIME: 5 MINUTES ■ **COOK TIME:** 5 MINUTES

 + + +

| 10 whole wheat *or* flour tortillas (6-inch) | 1 container (18 ounces) refrigerated cooked barbecue sauce with shredded pork (about 2 cups) | 1 cup Pace® Chunky Salsa | ¼ teaspoon ground chipotle chile pepper |

1. Heat the oven to 350°F. Spray 10 (3-inch) muffin-pan cups with vegetable cooking spray.

2. Wrap the tortillas between damp paper towels. Microwave on HIGH for 30 seconds or until the tortillas are warm. Fold **1** tortilla into thirds to form a cone shape. Press the tortilla cone, wide-end down, into a muffin-pan cup. Repeat with the remaining tortillas, rewarming in the microwave as needed.

3. Bake for 5 minutes or until the tortilla cones are golden. Remove the tortillas from the pan and cool on wire racks.

4. Heat the pork, salsa and chipotle chile pepper in a 2-quart saucepan over medium heat until the mixture is hot and bubbling, stirring often.

5. Spoon **about ¼ cup** pork mixture into each tortilla cone. Top with shredded Cheddar cheese, guacamole, sour cream or olives, if desired.

Grilled Beef Steak with Sautéed Onions

MAKES 8 SERVINGS ■ **PREP TIME:** 10 MINUTES ■ **COOK TIME:** 5 MINUTES
GRILL TIME: 20 MINUTES ■ **STAND TIME:** 5 MINUTES

 + + +

| 2 tablespoons olive oil | 2 large onions, thinly sliced (about 2 cups) | 1 jar (16 ounces) Pace® Chunky Salsa | 2-pound boneless beef sirloin steak, strip steak *or* rib steak |

1. Heat **1 tablespoon** oil in a 12-inch skillet over medium heat. Add the onions and cook until they're tender. Add **2½ cups** salsa and cook until heated through. Remove the onion mixture from the skillet and keep warm.

2. Lightly oil the grill rack and heat the grill to medium. Grill the steak for 20 minutes for medium-rare or to desired doneness, turning the steak over halfway through cooking and brushing often with remaining salsa. Discard any leftover salsa.

3. Let steak stand 5 minutes then cut into 8 pieces. Serve with the onion mixture.

■ **Kitchen Tip**

This recipe will work fine with almost any kind of onion.

Awesome Grilled Cheese Sandwiches

MAKES 3 SANDWICHES ■ **PREP TIME:** 10 MINUTES ■ **COOK TIME:** 5 MINUTES

| 1 package (11.25 ounces) Pepperidge Farm® Frozen Garlic Texas Toast | 6 slices fontina *or* fresh mozzarella cheese (about 6 ounces) | 6 thin slices deli smoked turkey | 3 thin slices prosciutto | 1 jar (12 ounces) sliced roasted red peppers, drained |

1. Heat a panini or sandwich press according to the manufacturer's directions until hot. (Or use a cast-iron skillet or ridged grill pan.)

2. Top **3** of the bread slices with **half** of the cheese, turkey, prosciutto, peppers and remaining cheese. Top with the remaining bread slices.

3. Put the sandwiches on the press, closing the lid onto the sandwiches. Cook the sandwiches for 5 minutes (if cooking in a skillet or grill pan, press with a spatula occasionally or weigh down with another cast-iron skillet/foil-covered brick), until they're lightly browned and the bread is crisp and the cheese melts.

■ Kitchen Tip

For a spicier flavor, add a dash of crushed red pepper flakes on the cheese when assembling the sandwiches.

Saucy Mario Sandwiches

MAKES 6 SERVINGS ■ **PREP TIME:** 5 MINUTES ■ **COOK TIME:** 15 MINUTES

 + + +

| 1 pound ground beef | 2 cups Prego® Traditional Italian Sauce, any variety | ¼ cup grated Parmesan cheese | 6 Pepperidge Farm® Classic Hamburger Buns, split |

1. Cook the beef in a 10-inch skillet over medium-high heat until the beef is well browned, stirring frequently to separate meat. Pour off any fat.

2. Stir the Italian sauce and cheese into the skillet. Cook until the mixture is hot and bubbling.

3. Divide the beef mixture among the buns.

Fettuccine Picante

MAKES 4 SERVINGS ■ **PREP TIME:** 15 MINUTES ■ **COOK TIME:** 5 MINUTES

 + + + +

| ½ cup Pace® Picante Sauce | ½ cup sour cream | ⅓ cup grated Parmesan cheese | ½ of a 1-pound package fettuccine, cooked and drained | 2 tablespoons chopped fresh cilantro leaves |

1. Heat the picante sauce, sour cream and cheese in a 2-quart saucepan over medium heat until the mixture is hot and bubbling.

2. Place the fettuccine and cilantro into a large serving bowl. Add the picante sauce mixture and toss to coat. Serve with additional picante sauce.

■ Kitchen Tip

You can use Pace® mild, medium or hot picante sauce in this recipe.

Baked Potatoes Olé

| 1 pound ground beef | + | 1 tablespoon chili powder | + | 1 cup Pace® Picante Sauce | + | 4 hot baked potatoes, split | + | Shredded Cheddar cheese |

1. Cook the beef and chili powder in a 10-inch skillet over medium-high heat until the beef is well browned, stirring often to separate meat. Pour off any fat.

2. Stir the picante sauce in the skillet. Reduce the heat to low. Cook until the mixture is hot and bubbling. Serve the beef mixture over the potatoes. Top with the cheese.

▪ Kitchen Tip

To bake the potatoes, pierce them with a fork and bake at 400°F. for 1 hour or microwave on HIGH for 12 minutes or until fork-tender.

French Onion Burgers

| 1 pound ground beef | 1 can (10½ ounces) Campbell's® Condensed French Onion Soup | 4 slices Swiss cheese | 4 round hard rolls, split |

1. Shape the beef into **4** (½-inch-thick) burgers.

2. Heat a 10-inch skillet over medium-high heat. Add the burgers and cook until they're well browned on both sides. Remove the burgers from the skillet. Pour off any fat.

3. Stir the soup in the skillet and heat to a boil. Return the burgers to the skillet. Reduce the heat to low. Cover and cook for 5 minutes or until the burgers are cooked through. Top the burgers with the cheese and cook until the cheese is melted. Serve the burgers on the rolls with the soup mixture.

■ Kitchen Tip

You can also serve these burgers in a bowl atop a mound of hot mashed potatoes, with some of the onion gravy poured over.

Pasta Primavera

 + + +

| 3 cups *uncooked* corkscrew-shaped pasta | 1 bag (16 ounces) frozen vegetable combination (broccoli, cauliflower, carrots) | 1 jar (1 pound 10 ounces) Prego® Traditional Italian Sauce, any variety | Grated Parmesan cheese |

1. Prepare pasta according to package directions in a 4-quart saucepan. Add the vegetables during the last 5 minutes of the cooking time. Drain the pasta and vegetables in a colander and return them to the saucepan.

2. Stir the Italian sauce into the saucepan. Heat, stirring occasionally, until hot and bubbling. Top with the cheese.

Buffalo Burgers

MAKES 4 SERVINGS ■ **PREP TIME:** 10 MINUTES ■ **COOK TIME:** 20 MINUTES

| 1 pound ground beef | + | 1 can (10¾ ounces) Campbell's® Condensed Tomato Soup (Regular *or* Healthy Request®) | + | ½ teaspoon Louisiana-style hot sauce | + | ½ cup crumbled blue cheese | + | 4 Pepperidge Farm® Classic Hamburger Buns, split |

1. Shape the beef into **4** (½-inch-thick) burgers.

2. Lightly oil the grill rack and heat the grill to medium. Grill the burgers for 10 minutes for medium or to desired doneness, turning the burgers over once halfway through grilling.

3. Heat the soup and hot sauce in a 1-quart saucepan over medium heat to a boil. Reduce the heat to low. Cover and cook for 5 minutes. Top the burgers with the soup mixture. Sprinkle with the cheese. Serve the burgers on the buns with lettuce, onion and tomato, if desired.

■ Kitchen Tip

Any leftover soup mixture can also be a great dipping sauce for French fries.

White Pizza Bagel Appetizers

MAKES 24 APPETIZERS ▪ **PREP TIME:** 15 MINUTES ▪ **BAKE TIME:** 10 MINUTES

| 1 package (17 ounces) Pepperidge Farm® Plain Mini Bagels, split | Garlic powder | 1 cup shredded mozzarella cheese (about 4 ounces) | ¼ cup sliced, pitted ripe olives | ¼ cup finely chopped green pepper *or* red pepper | ¼ teaspoon dried oregano leaves, crushed |

1. Heat the oven to 400°F. Place the bagel halves, cut-side up, on an ungreased baking sheet. Sprinkle with garlic powder. Bake for 5 minutes or until the bagels are lightly toasted.

2. Top the bagels with the cheese, olives, pepper and oregano. Bake for 5 minutes or until the cheese is melted.

▪ Kitchen Tip

You can serve these tasty bites with warm Prego® Traditional Italian Sauce for dipping.

Chicken Pesto & Pepper Sandwiches

MAKES 4 SANDWICHES ▪ **PREP TIME:** 10 MINUTES ▪ **GRILL TIME:** 15 MINUTES

| ½ cup prepared pesto sauce | 4 Pepperidge Farm® Classic Sandwich Buns with Sesame Seeds | 4 skinless, boneless chicken breast halves | 4 slices mozzarella cheese | 1 jar (7 ounces) roasted red peppers, drained |

1. Spread **about 1 teaspoon** pesto sauce on each bun half.

2. Lightly oil the grill rack and heat the grill to medium. Grill the chicken for 15 minutes or until it's cooked through, turning and brushing often with the remaining pesto sauce during the last 5 minutes of grilling.

3. Top the chicken with the cheese.

4. Layer the bottom bun halves with lettuce, if desired, chicken and roasted red peppers. Top with the remaining bun halves.

Cheesy Broccoli Potato Topper

MAKES 4 SERVINGS ■ **PREP TIME:** 10 MINUTES ■ **COOK TIME:** 4 MINUTES

1 can (10¾ ounces)
Campbell's® Condensed
Cheddar Cheese Soup

+

4 hot baked
potatoes, split

+

1 cup cooked
broccoli flowerets

1. Stir the soup in the can until it's smooth.

2. Place the potatoes onto a microwavable plate. Top with the broccoli. Spoon the soup over the broccoli.

3. Microwave on HIGH for 4 minutes or until the soup is hot.

Chicken Salsa Pockets

MAKES 6 SANDWICHES ■ **PREP TIME:** 5 MINUTES ■ **COOK TIME:** 10 MINUTES

| 1 can (10¾ ounces) Campbell's® Condensed Cream of Chicken Soup (Regular *or* 98% Fat Free) | ½ cup Pace® Chunky Salsa | 2 cups cooked chicken, cut into strips | ½ cup shredded Cheddar cheese | 3 pita breads (6-inch), cut in half, forming 2 pockets |

1. Stir the soup, salsa and chicken in a 2-quart saucepan. Cook and stir over medium heat until hot. Stir in the cheese. Cook until the cheese melts.

2. Line the pita halves with lettuce, if desired. Spoon **about ⅓ cup** chicken mixture into each pita half.

■ Kitchen Tip

*Substitute **2 cans** (4.5 ounces **each**) Swanson® Premium Chunk Chicken breast, drained, for the cooked chicken.*

Easy Beef & Pasta

MAKES 4 SERVINGS ▪ **PREP TIME:** 5 MINUTES ▪ **COOK TIME:** 20 MINUTES

 + + +

| 1 tablespoon vegetable oil | 1 pound boneless beef sirloin steak, ¾-inch thick, cut into very thin strips | 1 can (10¾ ounces) Campbell's® Condensed Tomato Soup (Regular *or* Healthy Request®) | 1 bag (about 16 ounces) frozen vegetable pasta blend |

1. Heat the oil in a 10-inch skillet over medium-high heat. Add the beef and cook until it's well browned, stirring often. Pour off any fat.

2. Stir the soup, ½ **cup** water and vegetable pasta blend in the skillet and heat to a boil. Reduce the heat to low. Cover and cook for 5 minutes or until the beef is cooked through.

Pizza Fries

| 1 bag (2 pounds) frozen French fries | 1 cup Prego® Traditional Italian Sauce, any variety | 1½ cups shredded mozzarella cheese (about 6 ounces) | Diced pepperoni, optional |

1. Prepare the fries according to the package directions. Remove from the oven. Pour the Italian sauce over the fries.

2. Top with the cheese and pepperoni, if desired.

3. Bake for 5 minutes or until the cheese is melted.

Quick Chicken Mozzarella Sandwiches

MAKES 4 SANDWICHES ▪ **PREP TIME:** 5 MINUTES ▪ **COOK TIME:** 15 MINUTES

 + + +

| 1 ½ cups Prego® Three Cheese Italian Sauce | 4 refrigerated *or* thawed frozen cooked breaded chicken cutlets | 4 slices mozzarella cheese | 4 round hard rolls |

1. Heat the Italian sauce in a 10-inch skillet over medium heat to a boil. Place the chicken in the sauce. Reduce the heat to low. Cover and cook for 5 minutes or until the chicken is heated through.

2. Top the chicken with the cheese. Cover and cook until the cheese is melted. Serve on the rolls.

Souper Sloppy Joes

MAKES 6 SANDWICHES ▪ **PREP TIME:** 5 MINUTES ▪ **COOK TIME:** 15 MINUTES

 + + +

| 1 pound ground beef | 1 can (10¾ ounces) Campbell's® Condensed Tomato Soup (Regular *or* Healthy Request®) | 1 tablespoon prepared yellow mustard | 6 Pepperidge Farm® Farmhouse Premium White Rolls with Sesame Seeds, split |

1. Cook the beef in a 10-inch skillet over medium-high heat until the beef is well browned, stirring frequently to separate the meat. Pour off any fat.

2. Stir the soup, ¼ **cup** water and mustard into the skillet. Cook and stir until the mixture is hot and bubbling.

3. Divide the beef mixture among the rolls.

Quick Cheesy Pizza

MAKES 6 SERVINGS ▪ **PREP TIME:** 10 MINUTES ▪ **BAKE TIME:** 10 MINUTES

 + +

| 1 package (14 ounces) prepared pizza crust (12-inch) | 1 cup Prego® Tomato, Basil & Garlic Italian Sauce | 1 cup shredded mozzarella cheese (4 ounces) |

1. Heat the oven to 450°F. Put the pizza crust on a 16-inch pizza pan or baking sheet.

2. Spread the Italian sauce over the crust to within ¼ inch of the edge. Top with the cheese.

3. Bake for 10 minutes or until the cheese melts and the crust is golden.

▪ Kitchen Tip

Add one or more of these toppings to your pizza before baking: Sliced pepperoni, chopped onions, green peppers, sliced mushrooms, minced fresh garlic and/or cooked crumbled sausage.

Chicken Quesadillas & Fiesta Rice

MAKES 10 QUESADILLAS ■ **PREP TIME:** 10 MINUTES ■ **BAKE TIME:** 5 MINUTES

 + + +

| 1 pound skinless, boneless chicken breasts, cubed | 1 can (10¾ ounces) Campbell's® Condensed Cheddar Cheese Soup | ½ cup Pace® Chunky Salsa *or* Picante Sauce | 10 flour tortillas (8-inch) |

1. Heat the oven to 425°F.

2. Spray a 10-inch skillet with cooking spray. Heat over medium-high heat for 1 minute. Add the chicken and cook until it's well browned, stirring often.

3. Stir the soup and salsa into the skillet. Cook until the mixture is hot and bubbling, stirring occasionally.

4. Put the tortillas on **2** baking sheets. Top **half** of **each** tortilla with **about** ⅓ **cup** soup mixture to within ½ inch of the edge. Moisten the edge of **each** tortilla with water. Fold over and press edges together to seal.

5. Bake for 5 minutes or until the filling is hot. Serve with *Fiesta Rice*.

■ Kitchen Tip

*For **Fiesta Rice**, heat **1 can** Campbell's® Condensed Chicken Broth, ½ **cup** water and ½ **cup** Pace® Chunky Salsa in a 2-quart saucepan over high heat to a boil. Stir in **2 cups uncooked** instant white rice. Cover and remove from the heat. Let stand 5 minutes, and then fluff the rice with a fork.*

Grilled Skewered Shrimp

| ⅔ cup Pace® Picante Sauce | 1 can (about 8 ounces) tomato sauce | 3 tablespoons packed brown sugar | 2 tablespoons lemon juice | 1½ pounds large shrimp, peeled and deveined |

1. Stir the picante sauce, tomato sauce, brown sugar and lemon juice in a large bowl. Add the shrimp and toss to coat.

2. Thread the shrimp on **12** skewers.

3. Lightly oil the grill rack and heat the grill to medium. Grill the shrimp for 10 minutes or until they're cooked through, turning and brushing often with the picante sauce mixture. Discard any remaining picante sauce mixture.

■ Kitchen Tip

For even easier preparation, you can buy frozen large shrimp already peeled and deveined. Just thaw and use instead of the fresh shrimp.

10-Minute Prep

An easy prep dish on busy nights provides a win-win solution to feeding your family.

Baked Crispy Chicken

MAKES 4 SERVINGS ■ **PREP TIME:** 10 MINUTES ■ **BAKE TIME:** 20 MINUTES

1. Stir ⅓ **cup** of the soup and ¼ **cup** of the milk in a shallow dish. Lightly coat the chicken with the flour. Dip the chicken into the soup mixture, then coat with the stuffing.

2. Put the chicken on a baking sheet. Drizzle with the butter. Bake at 400°F. for 20 minutes or until the chicken is cooked through.

3. Heat the remaining soup and milk in a 1-quart saucepan over medium heat until hot, stirring occasionally. Serve the sauce with the chicken.

 +
 +
 +

| 1 can (10¾ ounces) Campbell's® Condensed Cream of Chicken Soup (Regular *or* 98% Fat Free) | ½ cup milk | 4 skinless, boneless chicken breast halves |

2 tablespoons all-purpose flour

1½ cups Pepperidge Farm® Herb Seasoned Stuffing, finely crushed

2 tablespoons butter, melted

Grilled Picante BBQ Chicken

MAKES 6 SERVINGS ■ **PREP TIME:** 5 MINUTES ■ **GRILL TIME:** 15 MINUTES

 + +

¾ cup Pace® Picante Sauce   ¼ cup barbecue sauce   6 skinless, boneless chicken breast halves

1. Stir the picante sauce and barbecue sauce in a small bowl. Reserve ½ **cup** picante sauce mixture for grilling. Set aside remaining picante sauce mixture to serve with the chicken.

2. Lightly oil the grill rack and heat the grill to medium. Grill the chicken for 15 minutes or until it's cooked through, turning and brushing often with the reserved picante sauce mixture during grilling. Discard any remaining picante sauce mixture.

3. Serve the chicken with the remaining ½ **cup** picante sauce mixture.

■ Kitchen Tip

This simple basting sauce also makes a zesty dipping sauce for chicken wings or nuggets.

Chicken Pesto with Tomatoes

MAKES 4 SERVINGS ■ **PREP TIME:** 5 MINUTES ■ **COOK TIME:** 20 MINUTES

4 skinless, boneless chicken breast halves

1 can (10¾ ounces) Campbell's® Condensed Cream of Chicken Soup (Regular *or* 98% Fat Free)

⅓ cup prepared pesto sauce

1 can (about 14.5 ounces) diced tomatoes, undrained

1. Spray a 10-inch skillet with vegetable cooking spray and heat over medium-high heat for 1 minute. Add the chicken and cook for 10 minutes or until it's well browned on both sides. Remove the chicken from the skillet.

2. Stir the soup, ½ **cup** water, pesto and tomatoes in the skillet and heat to a boil. Return the chicken to the skillet. Reduce the heat to low. Cover and cook for 5 minutes or until the chicken is cooked through. Serve with hot cooked pasta, if desired.

Fontina Turkey Panini

MAKES 2 SANDWICHES ■ **PREP TIME:** 5 MINUTES ■ **COOK TIME:** 15 MINUTES

| 4 slices Pepperidge Farm® Farmhouse Sourdough Bread | 2 tablespoons honey mustard salad dressing | 4 slices fontina cheese | 2 slices smoked turkey | 4 bread-and-butter pickle sandwich slices |

1. Brush **1** side of the bread slices with olive oil.

2. Turn **2** bread slices oil-side down. Spread **each** with **1 tablespoon** salad dressing. Top **each** with **2** cheese slices, **1** turkey slice, **2** pickle slices and the remaining bread slices, oil-side up.

3. Heat a grill pan or skillet over medium heat. Add the sandwiches and cook for 4 minutes or until they're lightly browned on both sides and the cheese is melted.

■ Kitchen Tip

Try pressing down on the sandwiches with a spatula during cooking. It will help the different ingredients melt together.

Chicken Pizza Muffins

MAKES 8 OPEN-FACED SANDWICHES OR 4 SERVINGS
PREP TIME: 10 MINUTES ■ **COOK TIME:** 3 MINUTES

 + + +

4 English muffins, split and toasted	½ cup Prego® Chunky Garden Combination Italian Sauce	2 cans (4.5 ounces *each*) Swanson® Premium Chunk White Chicken, drained	¼ cup shredded part-skim mozzarella cheese

1. Heat the broiler. Put the muffin halves on a rack in a broiler pan.

2. Spread about **1 tablespoon** of the Italian sauce on **each** muffin half. Divide the chicken and cheese among the muffin halves. Sprinkle with red pepper, oregano or garlic powder, if desired.

3. Broil the sandwiches with the top of the cheese 4 inches from the heat for 3 minutes or until the cheese melts.

Tasty 2-Step Chicken

MAKES 6 SERVINGS ■ **PREP TIME:** 5 MINUTES ■ **COOK TIME:** 20 MINUTES

 +  +

| 1 tablespoon vegetable oil | 4 skinless, boneless chicken breast halves | 1 can (10¾ ounces) Campbell's® Condensed Cream of Mushroom Soup (Regular *or* 98% Fat Free) |

1. Heat the oil in a 10-inch skillet over medium-high heat. Add the chicken and cook for 10 minutes or until it's browned. Set the chicken aside. Pour off any fat.

2. Stir the soup and ½ **cup** water into the skillet. Heat to a boil. Return the chicken to the skillet and reduce the heat to low. Cover and cook for 5 minutes or until the chicken is cooked through.

Country Beef & Vegetables

MAKES 6 SERVINGS ■ **PREP TIME:** 5 MINUTES ■ **COOK TIME:** 20 MINUTES

| 1½ pounds ground beef | 1 can (26 ounces) Campbell's® Condensed Tomato Soup | 1 tablespoon Worcestershire sauce | 1 bag (16 ounces) frozen mixed vegetables | Shredded Cheddar cheese |

1. Cook the beef in a 10-inch skillet over medium-high heat until it's well browned, stirring frequently to separate meat. Pour off any fat.

2. Stir the soup, Worcestershire and vegetables into the skillet. Heat to a boil. Reduce the heat to low. Cover and cook for 5 minutes or until the vegetables are tender. Serve over hot cooked rice. Top with the cheese.

Chicken with Artichokes

MAKES 6 SERVINGS ■ **PREP TIME:** 10 MINUTES ■ **COOK TIME:** 20 MINUTES

 +  + + +

| 2 jars (6 ounces *each*) marinated artichoke hearts packed in oil | 6 skinless, boneless chicken breast halves | 1 jar (1 pound 10 ounces) Prego® Onion & Garlic *or* Traditional Italian Sauce | 6 slices prosciutto *or* salami (about 2 ounces) | 6 slices provolone cheese (about 4 ounces) |

1. Drain the artichokes, reserving **1 tablespoon** of the oil.

2. Heat the reserved oil in a 12-inch skillet over medium-high heat. Add the chicken and cook for 10 minutes or until it's well browned on both sides. Add the artichokes and cook for 1 minute.

3. Add the Italian sauce to the skillet and reduce the heat to medium. Cover and cook for 5 minutes or until the chicken is cooked through.

4. Top **each** chicken breast with **1** slice **each** prosciutto and cheese. Cover and cook for 2 minutes or until the cheese melts. Serve with hot cooked orzo.

Corn-Crusted Catfish

MAKES 6 SERVINGS ■ **PREP TIME:** 5 MINUTES
MARINATE TIME: 15 MINUTES ■ **COOK TIME:** 20 MINUTES

| 1½ cups buttermilk | 1 teaspoon hot pepper sauce | 6 fresh catfish fillets (6 ounces *each*) | 1½ to 2 cups crushed Pepperidge Farm® Cornbread Stuffing | Vegetable oil |

1. Stir the buttermilk and hot sauce in a shallow bowl. Add the catfish fillets and turn to coat with the buttermilk mixture. Let marinate for 15 minutes. Remove the fish from the marinade. Place the stuffing on a plate. Coat both sides of the fish with the stuffing.

2. Pour the oil into a deep, heavy skillet to a depth of ¼-inch. Heat to about 370°F. Add the fish in 2 batches and cook for 6 to 8 minutes, carefully turning once or until the fish flakes easily when tested with a fork. Remove with a pancake turner and drain on paper towels. Serve the fish with lemon wedges and tartar sauce.

■ **Kitchen Tip**

Place stuffing in resealable plastic bag and seal. Use a rolling pin and roll back and forth over bag until it's crushed.

Baked Pork Chops with Garden Stuffing

MAKES 6 SERVINGS ■ **PREP TIME:** 15 MINUTES ■ **BAKE TIME:** 40 MINUTES

| 1 can (10¾ ounces) Campbell's® Condensed Golden Mushroom Soup | 1 bag (16 ounces) frozen vegetable combination (broccoli, cauliflower, carrots) | 1 tablespoon butter | 4 cups Pepperidge Farm® Herb Seasoned Stuffing | 6 bone-in pork chops, ¾-inch thick |

1. Heat the oven to 400°F.

2. Heat ⅓ **cup** soup, ½ **cup** water, vegetables and butter in a 3-quart saucepan over medium heat to a boil. Remove the saucepan from the heat. Add the stuffing and mix lightly. Spoon the stuffing mixture into a greased 3-quart baking dish. Arrange the pork on the stuffing.

3. Stir the remaining soup and ¼ **cup** water in a small bowl. Spoon the soup mixture over the pork.

4. Bake for 40 minutes or until the pork is cooked through.

■ Kitchen Tip

You can try varying the vegetable combination or the stuffing flavor for a different spin on this recipe.

Pork Chops Parmesan

MAKES 6 SERVINGS ■ **PREP TIME:** 5 MINUTES
COOK TIME: 25 MINUTES ■ **STAND TIME:** 5 MINUTES

| 1 tablespoon olive oil | 6 boneless pork chops, ¾-inch thick | 1½ cups Prego® Traditional Italian Sauce | ¼ cup grated Parmesan cheese | 1½ cups shredded mozzarella cheese (6 ounces) |

1. Heat the oil in a 12-inch skillet over medium-high heat. Add the pork chops and cook until the chops are well browned on both sides.

2. Pour the Italian sauce and **3 tablespoons** Parmesan cheese into the skillet. Turn the chops to coat. Reduce the heat to medium. Cover and cook for 10 minutes or until the chops are cooked through.

3. Sprinkle the mozzarella cheese and remaining Parmesan cheese over the chops. Let stand for 5 minutes or until the cheese melts.

Saucy Pork Chops

MAKES 4 SERVINGS ■ **PREP TIME:** 5 MINUTES ■ **COOK TIME:** 20 MINUTES

 +  +

| 1 tablespoon vegetable oil | 4 bone-in pork chops, ½-inch thick | 1 can (10¾ ounces) Campbell's® Condensed Cream of Onion Soup |

1. Heat the oil in a 10-inch skillet over medium-high heat. Add the pork chops and cook until the chops are well browned on both sides.

2. Stir the soup and ¼ **cup** water into the skillet. Heat to a boil. Reduce the heat to low. Cover and cook for 10 minutes or until the chops are cooked through but slightly pink in center.

Sirloin Steak Picante

MAKES 6 SERVINGS ■ **PREP TIME:** 5 MINUTES
GRILL TIME: 20 MINUTES ■ **STAND TIME:** 10 MINUTES

  +

1½ pounds boneless beef sirloin
***or* top round steak, 1½-inch thick**

1 cup Pace® Picante Sauce
***or* Chunky Salsa**

1. Lightly oil the grill rack and heat the grill to medium.

2. Grill the steak for 20 minutes for medium or to desired doneness, turning the steak over once during grilling and brushing often with ½ **cup** of the picante sauce.

3. Let stand for 10 minutes before serving. Serve with additional picante sauce.

■ Kitchen Tip

The picante sauce keeps the meat moist during grilling and adds tons of flavor. Vary the heat level using the mild, medium or hot varieties.

One Dish, No Fuss

Minimal prep, easy clean-up and maximum results equal complete satisfaction.

Cheesy Chicken Bake

MAKES 4 SERVINGS ■ **PREP TIME:** 5 MINUTES ■ **BAKE TIME:** 40 MINUTES

1. Stir the soup, **1⅓ cups** water, Worcestershire, rice, chicken and cheese in a 2-quart casserole. **Cover**.

2. Bake at 350°F. for 35 minutes or until hot. Stir.

3. Sprinkle with onions. Bake for 5 minutes more or until golden.

\+

\+

\+

1 can (10¾ ounces) Campbell's® Condensed Cream of Chicken Soup (Regular *or* 98% Fat Free)

1 teaspoon Worcestershire sauce

¾ cup *uncooked* regular long-grain white rice

+

+

**2 cups cubed
cooked chicken**

**½ cup shredded
Cheddar cheese**

**1 can (2.8 ounces) French
fried onions (1⅓ cups)**

Fake 'em Out Ravioli Lasagna

MAKES 6 SERVINGS ▪ **PREP TIME:** 10 MINUTES
BAKE TIME: 45 MINUTES ▪ **STAND TIME:** 10 MINUTES

 +  +

| 3 cups Prego® Italian Sausage & Garlic Italian Sauce | 1 package (30 ounces) frozen regular-size cheese-filled ravioli (about 30 to 34) | 1½ cups shredded mozzarella cheese (about 6 ounces) |

1. Heat the oven to 375°F. Spray a 3-quart shallow baking dish with vegetable cooking spray.

2. Stir the Italian sauce and ½ **cup** water in a medium bowl. Spread **1 cup** sauce mixture in the baking dish. Top with ½ of the ravioli, ¾ **cup** mozzarella cheese and **1 cup** sauce mixture. Top with the remaining ravioli and sauce mixture. Cover the baking dish.

3. Bake for 35 minutes or until the mixture is hot and bubbling. Uncover the baking dish. Sprinkle with the remaining mozzarella cheese.

4. Bake for 10 minutes or until the cheese is melted. Let stand for 10 minutes. Garnish with Parmesan cheese and parsley, as desired.

Skillet Chicken Primavera

MAKES 4 SERVINGS ■ **PREP TIME:** 5 MINUTES ■ **COOK TIME:** 25 MINUTES

| 1 tablespoon vegetable oil | 4 skinless, boneless chicken breast halves | 1 jar (1 pound 10 ounces) Prego® Traditional Italian Sauce | 4 cups frozen vegetable combination (spinach, broccoli, carrots, red pepper) *or* (broccoli, cauliflower, carrots) | Grated Parmesan cheese |

1. Heat the oil in a 10-inch skillet over medium-high heat. Add the chicken and cook for 10 minutes or until it's well browned on both sides. Remove the chicken and set aside.

2. Stir the Italian sauce and vegetables into the skillet. Heat to a boil. Return the chicken to the skillet and reduce the heat to low. Cover and cook for 10 minutes or until the chicken is cooked through and the vegetables are tender. Sprinkle with the cheese.

Turkey & Tortellini Alfredo

MAKES 6 SERVINGS ■ **PREP TIME:** 5 MINUTES ■ **COOK TIME:** 15 MINUTES

| 1 pound Italian-style turkey sausage, casing removed | 1 can (10¾ ounces) Campbell's® Condensed Cream of Chicken Soup (Regular *or* 98% Fat Free) | 1 can (14.5 ounces) diced tomatoes, undrained | 1 pound (16 ounces) frozen cheese-filled tortellini | 2 tablespoons chopped fresh basil leaves |

1. Cook the sausage in a 10-inch skillet over medium-high heat until it's well browned, stirring frequently to separate meat. Pour off any fat.

2. Stir the soup, ½ **cup** water and tomatoes with juice into the skillet. Heat to a boil. Add the tortellini and reduce the heat to low. Cook for about 5 minutes or until the tortellini is tender but still firm.

3. Stir in the basil. Serve with grated Parmesan cheese, if desired.

Enchilada-Style Casserole

| 2 cans (10¾ ounces *each*) Campbell's® Condensed Cheddar Cheese Soup | 1 jar (16 ounces) Pace® Chunky Salsa | 4 cups cubed cooked chicken | 8 flour *or* 12 corn tortillas (6- to 8-inch), cut into strips | 1 cup shredded Cheddar cheese (4 ounces) |

1. Mix the soup, ½ **cup** water, ½ **cup** salsa and chicken in a 3-quart bowl. Stir in the tortillas. Spread the chicken mixture in a 13×9×2-inch shallow baking dish. Top with the cheese. **Cover**.

2. Bake at 350°F. for 35 minutes or until hot and bubbling. Serve with the remaining salsa.

Sloppy Joe Casserole

MAKES 5 SERVINGS ■ **PREP TIME:** 15 MINUTES ■ **BAKE TIME:** 15 MINUTES

| 1 pound ground beef | 1 can (10¾ ounces) Campbell's® Condensed Tomato Soup (Regular *or* Healthy Request®) | 1 teaspoon Worcestershire sauce | 1 package (7.5 ounces) refrigerated biscuits (10 biscuits) | ½ cup shredded Cheddar cheese |

1. Heat the oven to 400°F.

2. Cook the beef in a 10-inch skillet over medium-high heat until it's well browned, stirring often to separate meat. Pour off any fat.

3. Stir the soup, ¼ **cup** water, Worcestershire and ⅛ **teaspoon** ground black pepper in the skillet and heat to a boil. Spoon the beef mixture into a 1½-quart casserole. Arrange the biscuits around the inside edge of the casserole.

4. Bake for 15 minutes or until the biscuits are golden brown. Sprinkle the cheese over the beef mixture.

■ Kitchen Tip

*Sharp **or** mild Cheddar cheese will work in this recipe.*

Chicken Scampi and Rice Bake

MAKES 4 SERVINGS ■ **PREP TIME:** 10 MINUTES ■ **BAKE TIME:** 40 MINUTES

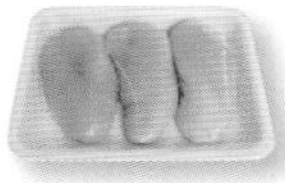

1 can (10¾ ounces) Campbell's® Condensed Cream of Chicken Soup (Regular _or_ 98% Fat Free)	**2 tablespoons lemon juice**	**3 cloves garlic, minced _or_ ¾ teaspoon garlic powder**	**¾ cup _uncooked_ regular long-grain white rice**	**4 skinless, boneless chicken breast halves**

1. Stir the soup, **1⅓ cups** water, lemon juice, garlic and rice in an 11×8-inch (2-quart) shallow baking dish. Top with the chicken. **Cover.**

2. Bake at 400°F. for 40 minutes or until the chicken is cooked through. Stir the mixture before serving. Garnish with lemon slices, as desired.

Baked Chicken & Broccoli

MAKES 8 SERVINGS ■ **PREP TIME:** 15 MINUTES ■ **COOK TIME:** 30 MINUTES

  + +   +

| 1 pound broccoli, trimmed, cut into 1-inch pieces, cooked and drained | 8 skinless, boneless chicken breast halves | 1 can (26 ounces) Campbell's® Condensed Cream of Mushroom Soup (Regular *or* 98% Fat Free) | ⅔ cup milk |

1. Place the broccoli and chicken in 13×9×2-inch (3-quart) shallow baking dish. Stir the soup, milk and ¼ **teaspoon** ground black pepper in a small bowl. Pour the soup mixture over the broccoli and chicken.

2. Bake at 400°F. for 30 minutes or until the chicken is cooked through. Stir the sauce before serving. Serve with hot cooked rice.

■ Kitchen Tip

*Substitute **1 bag** (16 ounces) frozen broccoli cuts, thawed and drained for fresh. To thaw broccoli, microwave on HIGH for 5 minutes.*

Beef Taco Skillet

| 1 pound ground beef | 1 can (10¾ ounces) Campbell's® Condensed Tomato Soup (Regular *or* Healthy Request®) | ½ cup Pace® Chunky Salsa | 6 flour tortillas (6-inch), cut into 1-inch pieces | ½ cup shredded Cheddar cheese |

1. Cook the beef in a 10-inch skillet over medium-high heat until it's well browned, stirring often to separate meat. Pour off any fat.

2. Stir the soup, salsa, ½ **cup** water and tortillas in the skillet and heat to a boil. Reduce the heat to low. Cook for 5 minutes. Stir the beef mixture. Top with the cheese.

Cheeseburger Chowder

MAKES 8 SERVINGS ■ **PREP TIME:** 10 MINUTES ■ **COOK TIME:** 20 MINUTES

1. Cook the beef and onion in a 3-quart saucepan over medium-high heat until the beef is well browned, stirring often to separate the meat. Pour off any fat.

2. Stir the soup and milk in the saucepan. Cook until the mixture is hot and bubbling. Stir in ½ **cup** cheese. Cook and stir until the cheese is melted.

3. Divide the soup among **8** serving bowls. Top **each** bowl with **1 tablespoon** remaining cheese and **2 tablespoons** croutons.

 +   +   +

| 1 pound ground beef | 1 large onion, chopped (about 1 cup) | 2 cans (26 ounces *each*) Campbell's® Condensed Cream of Mushroom Soup (Regular *or* 98% Fat Free) |

 + +

| 2 soup cans milk | 1 cup finely shredded Cheddar cheese (about 4 ounces) | 1 cup Pepperidge Farm® Seasoned Croutons |

Cacciatore Noodle Casserole

MAKES 6 SERVINGS ▪ **PREP TIME:** 10 MINUTES ▪ **BAKE TIME:** 25 MINUTES

1. Stir the Italian sauce, ¾ **cup** water, Italian vegetables, mushrooms, chicken and noodles in a 2-quart casserole.

2. Bake at 400°F. for 25 minutes or until hot. Stir.

3. Sprinkle with the cheese.

▪ Kitchen Tip

*Substitute leftover cubed rotisserie chicken **or 2 cans** (12.5 ounces **each**) Swanson® Premium White Chunk Chicken Breast, drained.*

 +  + +

| 2 cups Prego® Traditional Italian Sauce | 1 cup frozen Italian-style vegetable combination | 1 jar (4.5 ounces) sliced mushrooms, drained |

+

+

**3 cups cubed
cooked chicken**

**3 cups medium
egg noodles,
cooked and drained**

**¼ cup grated
Parmesan cheese**

Pennsylvania Dutch Ham & Noodle Casserole

MAKES 4 SERVINGS ■ **PREP TIME:** 10 MINUTES ■ **COOK TIME:** 15 MINUTES

1. Heat the oil in a 4-quart saucepan over medium-high heat. Add the ham and onion and cook until the onion is tender.

2. Stir the soup into the saucepan. Reduce the heat to medium. Cook and stir for 5 minutes. Add the cheese and stir until the cheese melts. Gently stir in the noodles. Heat through, stirring often.

■ Kitchen Tip

*Substitute cooked chicken **or** turkey for the ham.*

 + + +

1 tablespoon vegetable oil

2 cups cubed cooked ham (about 1 pound)

1 medium onion, chopped (about ½ cup)

1 can (10¾ ounces) Campbell's® Condensed Cream of Mushroom Soup (Regular *or* 98% Fat Free)

8 ounces extra-sharp Cheddar cheese, sliced

8 ounces extra-wide egg noodles (2 cups), cooked and drained

Zucchini, Chicken & Rice Casserole

MAKES 4 SERVINGS ■ **PREP TIME:** 15 MINUTES
BAKE TIME: 35 MINUTES ■ **STAND TIME:** 10 MINUTES

1. Heat the oven to 375°F. Spray a 3-quart shallow baking dish with vegetable cooking spray.

2. Stir the chicken, zucchini, peppers and rice in the baking dish.

3. Stir the soup, **1 soup can** water and sour cream in a small bowl. Pour the soup mixture over the chicken mixture. Cover the baking dish.

4. Bake for 35 minutes or until the rice is tender. Let stand for 10 minutes. Stir the rice before serving.

■ Kitchen Tip

Choose zucchini that have firm, dark green skin.

 + + +

1 package (12 ounces) refrigerated *or* thawed frozen breaded cooked chicken tenders, cut into bite-sized strips	2 large zucchini, cut in half lengthwise and thinly sliced (about 4 cups)	1 jar (7 ounces) whole roasted sweet peppers, drained and thinly sliced

 + +

1 cup **uncooked** instant brown rice

1 can (10¾ ounces) Campbell's® Condensed Cream of Celery Soup (Regular **or** 98% Fat Free)

½ cup sour cream

Tuscan Sausage and Rigatoni

MAKES 8 SERVINGS ■ **PREP TIME:** 5 MINUTES ■ **COOK TIME:** 20 MINUTES

1. Cook the sausage in a 10-inch skillet over medium-high heat until it's well browned, stirring often to separate the meat. Pour off any fat.

2. Stir the mushrooms and peas in the skillet. Cook for 5 minutes or until the mushrooms are tender, stirring often.

3. Stir the Italian sauce in the skillet. Reduce the heat to medium. Cook until the mixture is hot and bubbling, stirring occasionally.

4. Place the pasta into a large serving bowl. Pour the sausage mixture over the pasta and toss to coat. Top with the cheese.

 + + +

1 pound sweet *or* hot Italian pork sausage, casing removed

1 package (8 ounces) sliced mushrooms

1 cup frozen peas

2⅔ cups Prego® Traditional
Italian Sauce

16 ounces large
tube-shaped pasta
(rigatoni), cooked and
drained

⅓ cup grated
Parmesan cheese

Quick Chicken Noodle Bake

MAKES 4 SERVINGS ■ **PREP TIME:** 10 MINUTES ■ **BAKE TIME:** 30 MINUTES

1. Stir the soup, milk, peas, chicken and noodles in a 1½-quart casserole.

2. Bake at 400°F. for 15 minutes. Stir.

3. Top with bread crumbs. Bake for 15 minutes more or until hot.

■ Kitchen Tip

*Substitute **1 can** (12.5 ounces) Swanson® Premium White Chunk Chicken Breast, drained, for the turkey **or** chicken in this recipe.*

1 can (10¾ ounces) Campbell's® Condensed Cream of Mushroom Soup (Regular *or* 98% Fat Free)

½ cup milk

1 cup cooked peas

 + +

**2 cups cubed
cooked chicken**

**2 cups medium
egg noodles, cooked
and drained**

**⅓ cup dry
bread crumbs**

Turkey and Stuffing Casserole

MAKES 6 SERVINGS ■ **PREP TIME:** 5 MINUTES ■ **BAKE TIME:** 25 MINUTES

1. Spray a 12×8×2-inch shallow baking dish with vegetable cooking spray and set aside.

2. Stir the soup and milk in a large bowl. Stir in the vegetables, turkey and stuffing. Spoon the mixture into the prepared dish.

3. Bake at 400°F. for 20 minutes or until hot and bubbling. Stir.

4. Sprinkle the cheese over the turkey mixture. Bake for 5 minutes more or until the cheese melts.

■ Kitchen Tip

*Substitute **1 can** (12.5 ounces) Swanson® Premium White Chunk Chicken Breast, drained, for the turkey **or** chicken in this recipe.*

 + + +

1 can (10¾ ounces) Campbell's® Condensed Cream of Mushroom Soup (Regular *or* 98% Fat Free)

1 cup milk *or* water

1 bag (16 ounces) frozen vegetable combination (broccoli, cauliflower, carrots), thawed

2 cups cubed cooked turkey *or* chicken

+

4 cups Pepperidge Farm® Cubed Herb Seasoned Stuffing

+

1 cup shredded Swiss *or* Cheddar cheese (4 ounces)

Penne with Creamy Vodka Sauce

MAKES 4 SERVINGS ■ **PREP TIME:** 5 MINUTES ■ **COOK TIME:** 20 MINUTES

1. Heat the Italian sauce, vodka, basil and pepper in a 3-quart saucepan over medium heat. Heat to a boil. Remove from the heat and stir in the cream.

2. Put the pasta in a large serving bowl. Pour the sauce mixture over the pasta. Toss to coat. Serve with the cheese, as desired.

■ Kitchen Tip

For a heartier meal, serve with a sautéed chicken breast.

 + + + +

| 2 jars (1 pound 10 ounces *each*) Prego® Chunky Tomato, Onion & Garlic Italian Sauce | ¼ cup vodka | ⅓ cup chopped fresh basil leaves | ¼ teaspoon crushed red pepper |

 ½ cup heavy cream

\+

 1 package (16 ounces) medium tube-shaped pasta (penne), cooked and drained

\+

 Grated Parmesan cheese

Steak & Mushroom Florentine

MAKES 4 SERVINGS ■ **PREP TIME:** 5 MINUTES ■ **COOK TIME:** 20 MINUTES

1. Heat **1 tablespoon** oil in a 10-inch skillet over medium-high heat. Add the beef and cook until it's well browned, stirring often. Remove the beef from the skillet. Pour off any fat.

2. Reduce the heat to medium. Add the remaining oil to the skillet. Add the onion and cook until it's tender-crisp. Add the spinach and cook until the spinach is wilted.

3. Stir the soup and **1 cup** water in the skillet and heat to a boil. Return the beef to the skillet. Reduce the heat to low. Cook until the mixture is hot and bubbling. Serve the beef mixture over the tomato. Season with ground black pepper.

   + +

| 2 tablespoons vegetable oil | 1 pound beef sirloin steak *or* beef top round steak, ¾-inch thick, cut into thin strips | 1 small onion, sliced (about ¼ cup) |

 + +

4 cups fresh baby spinach leaves

1 can (10¾ ounces) Campbell's® Condensed Cream of Mushroom Soup (Regular *or* 98% Fat Free)

1 large tomato, thickly sliced

Skillet Lasagna

MAKES 4 SERVINGS ■ **PREP TIME:** 15 MINUTES ■ **COOK TIME:** 10 MINUTES

1. Cook the beef in a 12-inch skillet over medium-high heat until it's well browned, stirring frequently to break up meat. Pour off any fat.

2. Stir the Italian sauce, cheeses and noodles into the skillet. Reduce the heat to medium. Cook and stir until hot and bubbling. Serve with additional Parmesan cheese.

■ Kitchen Tip

For meatier skillet lasagna, substitute Prego® Italian Sausage & Garlic Italian Sauce for the Prego® Traditional Italian Sauce.

 +   +   +

1 pound **ground beef**	**1 jar (1 pound 10 ounces)** **Prego® Traditional** **Italian Sauce**	**½ cup** **ricotta cheese**

 +   +

½ cup shredded
mozzarella cheese

¼ cup grated
Parmesan cheese

4 cups medium
egg noodles,
cooked and drained

Penne Puttanesca

MAKES 4 SERVINGS ▪ **PREP TIME:** 10 MINUTES ▪ **COOK TIME:** 10 MINUTES

1. Spray a 10-inch skillet with vegetable cooking spray. Heat over medium-high heat for 1 minute. Add the olives, capers and red pepper. Cook for 2 minutes, stirring often. Stir the Italian sauce and **2 tablespoons** of the cheese into the skillet. Heat to a boil.

2. Stir the pasta into the skillet. Heat, stirring occasionally, until hot and bubbling. Top with the remaining cheese.

 + + +

½ cup kalamata olives, drained, pitted and chopped

1 tablespoon capers, drained

¼ teaspoon crushed red pepper

2 cups Prego® Tomato,
Basil & Garlic Italian Sauce

¼ cup grated
Parmesan cheese

½ of a 16-ounce package
tube-shaped pasta
(penne), cooked and
drained

Creamy Tortellini with Chicken

MAKES 4 SERVINGS ▪ **PREP TIME:** 15 MINUTES ▪ **BAKE TIME:** 20 MINUTES

1. Stir the Italian sauce and half-and-half in an 11×8-inch (2-quart) shallow baking dish.

2. Add the tortellini, chicken and **½ cup** of the mozzarella cheese. Stir well to coat. Top with the Parmesan cheese and remaining mozzarella cheese.

3. Bake at 400°F. for 20 minutes or until hot.

▪ Kitchen Tip

*Substitute **1 cup** coarsely chopped mushrooms and Prego® Traditional Sauce for the Prego® Fresh Mushroom Italian Sauce.*

 + + +

2 cups Prego® Fresh Mushroom Italian Sauce

⅓ cup half-and-half

1 package (16 ounces) frozen cheese-filled tortellini, cooked and drained

 + +

2 cups cooked chicken strips   **1 cup shredded mozzarella cheese (4 ounces)**   **¼ cup grated Parmesan cheese**

Garlic Mashed Potatoes & Beef Bake

MAKES 4 SERVINGS ▪ **PREP TIME:** 15 MINUTES ▪ **BAKE TIME:** 20 MINUTES

1. Heat the oven to 400°F. Cook the beef in a 10-inch skillet over medium-high heat until it's well browned, stirring often to separate meat. Pour off any fat.

2. Stir the beef, ½ **can** soup, Worcestershire and vegetables in a 2-quart shallow baking dish.

3. Heat **2 cups** water, butter and remaining soup in a 3-quart saucepan over medium heat to a boil. Remove the saucepan from the heat. Stir in the milk. Stir in the potatoes. Spoon the potatoes over the beef mixture.

4. Bake for 20 minutes or until the potatoes are lightly browned.

▪ Kitchen Tip

You can use your favorite frozen vegetable combination in this recipe.

    +   +   +

1 pound **ground beef**	**1 can (10¾ ounces)** **Campbell's® Condensed** **Cream of Mushroom with** **Roasted Garlic Soup**	**1 tablespoon** **Worcestershire sauce**

 + + +

| 1 bag (16 ounces) frozen vegetable combination (broccoli, cauliflower, carrots), thawed | 3 tablespoons butter | ¾ cup milk | 2 cups instant mashed potato flakes |

Chicken & Roasted Garlic Risotto

MAKES 4 SERVINGS ■ **PREP TIME:** 5 MINUTES
COOK TIME: 20 MINUTES ■ **STAND TIME:** 5 MINUTES

1. Season the chicken as desired.

2. Heat the butter in a 10-inch skillet over medium-high heat. Add the chicken and cook for 10 minutes or until it's well browned on both sides. Remove the chicken from the skillet.

3. Stir the soups and **2 cups** water in the skillet and heat to a boil. Stir in the rice and vegetables. Return the chicken to the skillet. Reduce the heat to low. Cover and cook for 5 minutes or until the chicken is cooked through. Remove the skillet from the heat. Let stand for 5 minutes.

■ Kitchen Tip

Traditionally, risotto is made by sautéing rice in butter then stirring broth into the rice a little at a time—very labor-intensive. This dish gives you the same creamy texture with a lot less work!

 + + +

4 skinless, boneless
chicken breast halves

1 tablespoon
butter

1 can (10¾ ounces)
Campbell's® Condensed
Cream of Chicken Soup
(Regular *or* 98% Fat Free)

1 can (10¾ ounces)
Campbell's® Condensed
Cream of Mushroom with
Roasted Garlic Soup

+

2 cups *uncooked*
instant white rice

+

1 cup frozen
peas and carrots

Spinach Ricotta Gnocchi

MAKES 6 SERVINGS ■ **PREP TIME:** 5 MINUTES ■ **COOK TIME:** 25 MINUTES

1. Prepare the gnocchi according to the package directions in a 6-quart saucepot. Add the spinach during the last 3 minutes of cooking. Drain the gnocchi mixture well in a colander. Return the gnocchi mixture to the saucepot.

2. Stir the Italian sauce, Romano cheese and ricotta cheese in the saucepot. Cook over medium heat until the mixture is hot and bubbling, stirring occasionally. Top with the mozzarella cheese.

■ Kitchen Tip

This dish is perfect for your next potluck dinner.

 + + +

1 package (16 ounces) frozen dumpling-shaped pasta (gnocchi)	**2 cups frozen cut-leaf spinach, thawed and well drained**	**1½ cups Prego® Heart Smart Onion & Garlic Italian Sauce *or* Prego® Traditional Italian Sauce**

 + +

**¼ cup grated
Romano cheese**   **½ cup
ricotta cheese**   **1 cup shredded
mozzarella cheese
(about 4 ounces)**

Dinner Winners

Family-pleasing favorites requested again and again.

Cheesy Tuna Noodle Casserole

MAKES 4 SERVINGS ▪ **PREP TIME:** 10 MINUTES ▪ **BAKE TIME:** 22 MINUTES

1. Stir the soup, milk, peas, tuna and noodles in a 1½-quart casserole.

2. Bake at 400°F. for 20 minutes or until hot. Stir.

3. Sprinkle cheese over the tuna mixture. Bake for 2 minutes more or until the cheese melts.

▪ Kitchen Tip

Substitute your family's favorite frozen vegetable for the peas.

 + + +

| 1 can (10¾ ounces) Campbell's® Condensed Cream of Mushroom Soup (Regular *or* 98% Fat Free) | ½ cup milk | 1 cup frozen peas |

  + +

2 cans
(about 6 ounces *each*)
tuna, drained and flaked

2 cups hot cooked
medium egg noodles

½ cup shredded
Cheddar cheese

Italian Sausage Sandwiches

MAKES 4 SANDWICHES ■ **PREP TIME:** 5 MINUTES ■ **COOK TIME:** 15 MINUTES

 + +

| 1 pound Italian pork sausage, casing removed | 1½ cups Prego® Chunky Garden Mushroom & Green Pepper Italian Sauce | 4 long hard rolls, split |

1. Cook the sausage in a 10-inch skillet over medium-high heat until it's well browned, stirring often to separate meat. Pour off any fat.

2. Stir in the Italian sauce and cook until the mixture is hot and bubbling. Serve the sausage mixture on the rolls.

■ Kitchen Tip

You can use your favorite Prego® Italian Sauce in this recipe.

Sensational Chicken Noodle Soup

MAKES 4 SERVINGS ▪ **PREP TIME:** 5 MINUTES ▪ **COOK TIME:** 20 MINUTES

4 cups Swanson® Chicken Broth (Regular, Natural Goodness® *or* Certified Organic)	1 medium carrot, sliced (about ½ cup)	1 stalk celery, sliced (about ½ cup)	½ cup *uncooked* medium egg noodles	1 cup cubed cooked chicken *or* turkey

1. Heat the broth, generous dash of ground black pepper, carrot and celery in a 2-quart saucepan over medium-high heat to a boil.

2. Stir in the noodles and chicken. Reduce the heat to medium. Cook for 10 minutes or until the noodles are tender but still firm.

Presto Parmesan

MAKES 6 SERVINGS ■ **PREP TIME:** 5 MINUTES ■ **BAKE TIME:** 25 MINUTES

 + + +

| 2¾ cups Prego® Traditional Italian Sauce | 6 frozen cooked breaded chicken breast fillets | 2 tablespoons grated Parmesan cheese | 1 cup shredded mozzarella cheese (4 ounces) |

1. Pour **1 cup** of the Italian sauce in a 13×9-inch (3-quart) shallow baking dish. Top with the chicken, remaining sauce and cheeses. **Cover**.

2. Bake at 400°F. for 20 minutes. Uncover and bake 5 minutes more or until the cheese is lightly browned.

■ Kitchen Tip

*To make Presto Pizza Parmesan, top the chicken with ½ **cup** chopped pepperoni before baking.*

Baked Macaroni & Cheese

| 1 can (10¾ ounces) Campbell's® Condensed Cheddar Cheese Soup | ½ soup can milk | 2 cups hot cooked corkscrew *or* medium shell macaroni (about 1½ cups *uncooked*) | 1 tablespoon dry bread crumbs | 2 teaspoons butter, melted |

1. Stir the soup, milk, ⅛ **teaspoon** ground black pepper and pasta in a 1-quart casserole.

2. Mix the bread crumbs with the butter in a small bowl. Sprinkle over the pasta mixture.

3. Bake at 400°F. for 20 minutes or until hot.

■ Kitchen Tips

*Double all ingredients, except increase butter to **1 tablespoon**, use 2-quart casserole and increase baking time to 25 minutes.*

*Substitute **2 cups** hot cooked elbow macaroni (**about 1 cup uncooked**) for corkscrew **or** shell macaroni.*

Creamy 3-Cheese Pasta

MAKES 4 SERVINGS ■ **PREP TIME:** 20 MINUTES ■ **BAKE TIME:** 20 MINUTES

| 1 can (10¾ ounces) Campbell's® Condensed Cream of Mushroom Soup (Regular *or* 98% Fat Free) | 1 cup milk | 1 package (8 ounces) shredded two-cheese blend | ⅓ cup grated Parmesan cheese | 3 cups corkscrew-shaped pasta (rotelle), cooked and drained |

1. Stir the soup, milk, ¼ **teaspoon** ground black pepper and cheeses in a 1½-quart casserole dish. Stir in the pasta.

2. Bake at 400°F. for 20 minutes or until hot.

3. Stir before serving.

One-Dish Chicken & Rice Bake

MAKES 4 SERVINGS ■ **PREP TIME:** 5 MINUTES ■ **BAKE TIME:** 45 MINUTES

| 1 can (10¾ ounces) Campbell's® Condensed Cream of Mushroom Soup (Regular *or* 98% Fat Free) | ¾ cup *uncooked* regular long-grain white rice | ¼ teaspoon paprika | 4 skinless, boneless chicken breast halves |

1. Stir the soup, **1⅓ cups** water, rice, paprika and ¼ **teaspoon** ground black pepper in an 11×8-inch (2-quart) shallow baking dish. Top with the chicken. Sprinkle the chicken with additional paprika and black pepper. **Cover**.

2. Bake at 375°F. for 45 minutes or until the chicken is cooked through and the rice is tender.

Mozzarella Meatball Sandwiches

MAKES 4 SANDWICHES ■ **PREP TIME:** 5 MINUTES
BAKE TIME: 10 MINUTES ■ **COOK TIME:** 20 MINUTES

 + +

| 1 loaf (11.75 ounces) Pepperidge Farm® Frozen Mozzarella & Garlic Cheese Bread | ½ cup Prego® Traditional *or* Organic Tomato & Basil Italian Sauce | 12 (½-ounce *each*) frozen meatballs *or* 6 (1-ounce *each*) frozen meatballs |

1. Heat the oven to 400°F.

2. Remove the bread from the bag. Place the frozen bread halves, cut-side up, on an ungreased baking sheet. (If bread halves are frozen together, carefully insert fork between halves to separate.) Place baking sheet on the middle oven rack. Bake for 10 minutes or until it's hot.

3. Heat the Italian sauce and meatballs in a 2-quart saucepan over low heat. Cook and stir for 20 minutes or until the meatballs are heated through.

4. Place the meatballs onto bottom bread half. Top with remaining bread half. Cut into quarters.

Easy Skillet Chicken Parmesan

MAKES 6 SERVINGS ■ **PREP TIME:** 5 MINUTES
COOK TIME: 15 MINUTES ■ **STAND TIME:** 5 MINUTES

| 1 tablespoon olive oil | 6 skinless, boneless chicken breast halves | 1½ cups Prego® Traditional Italian Sauce *or* Prego® Organic Tomato & Basil Italian Sauce | ¼ cup grated Parmesan cheese | 1½ cups shredded mozzarella cheese (about 6 ounces) |

1. Heat the oil in a 12-inch skillet over medium-high heat. Add the chicken and cook for 10 minutes or until it's well browned on both sides.

2. Stir the Italian sauce and **3 tablespoons** Parmesan cheese in the skillet. Reduce the heat to medium. Cover and cook for 5 minutes or until the chicken is cooked through.

3. Sprinkle the mozzarella cheese and remaining Parmesan cheese over the chicken. Let stand for 5 minutes or until the cheese is melted.

Cheeseburger Pasta

MAKES 5 SERVINGS ■ **PREP TIME:** 5 MINUTES ■ **COOK TIME:** 20 MINUTES

 + + +

| 1 pound ground beef | 1 can (10¾ ounces) Campbell's® Condensed Cheddar Cheese Soup | 1 can (10¾ ounces) Campbell's® Condensed Tomato Soup (Regular *or* Healthy Request®) | 2 cups *uncooked* medium shell-shaped pasta |

1. Cook the beef in a 10-inch skillet over medium-high heat until it's well browned, stirring often to separate meat. Pour off any fat.

2. Stir the soups, **1½ cups** water and pasta in the skillet and heat to a boil. Reduce the heat to medium. Cook for 10 minutes or until the pasta is tender, stirring often.

Spicy Salsa Mac & Beef

MAKES 4 SERVINGS ■ **PREP TIME:** 5 MINUTES ■ **COOK TIME:** 20 MINUTES

| 1 pound ground beef | 1 can (10½ ounces) Campbell's® Condensed Beef Broth | 2 cups *uncooked* medium shell-shaped pasta | 1 can (10¾ ounces) Campbell's® Condensed Cheddar Cheese Soup | 1 cup Pace® Chunky Salsa |

1. Cook the beef in a 10-inch skillet over medium-high heat until the beef is well browned, stirring frequently to separate meat. Pour off any fat.

2. Stir the broth and **1⅓ cups** water into the skillet. Heat to a boil. Add the pasta. Reduce the heat to medium. Cook and stir for 10 minutes or until the pasta is tender but still firm.

3. Stir the soup and salsa into the skillet. Cook and stir until hot and bubbling.

Sloppy Joe Pizza

MAKES 4 SERVINGS ■ **PREP TIME:** 10 MINUTES
COOK TIME: 10 MINUTES ■ **BAKE TIME:** 12 MINUTES

 + +

| ¾ pound ground beef | 1 can (10¾ ounces) Campbell's® Condensed Tomato Soup (Regular *or* Healthy Request®) | 1 Italian bread shell (12-inch) | 1½ cups shredded Cheddar cheese (6 ounces) |

1. Heat the oven to 450°F.

2. Cook the beef in a 10-inch skillet over medium-high heat until the beef is well browned, stirring frequently to separate meat. Pour off any fat.

3. Stir the soup into the skillet. Reduce the heat to low and cook until the mixture is hot and bubbling.

4. Spread the beef mixture over the shell to within ¼ inch of the edge. Top with the cheese.

5. Bake for 12 minutes or until the cheese melts.

Index

26

Index

70

62

Metric Chart

VOLUME MEASUREMENTS (dry)

$^1/_8$ teaspoon = 0.5 mL
$^1/_4$ teaspoon = 1 mL
$^1/_2$ teaspoon = 2 mL
$^3/_4$ teaspoon = 4 mL
1 teaspoon = 5 mL
1 tablespoon = 15 mL
2 tablespoons = 30 mL
$^1/_4$ cup = 60 mL
$^1/_3$ cup = 75 mL
$^1/_2$ cup = 125 mL
$^2/_3$ cup = 150 mL
$^3/_4$ cup = 175 mL
1 cup = 250 mL
2 cups = 1 pint = 500 mL
3 cups = 750 mL
4 cups = 1 quart = 1 L

VOLUME MEASUREMENTS (fluid)

1 fluid ounce (2 tablespoons) = 30 mL
4 fluid ounces ($^1/_2$ cup) = 125 mL
8 fluid ounces (1 cup) = 250 mL
12 fluid ounces (1$^1/_2$ cups) = 375 mL
16 fluid ounces (2 cups) = 500 mL

WEIGHTS (mass)

$^1/_2$ ounce = 15 g
1 ounce = 30 g
3 ounces = 90 g
4 ounces = 120 g
8 ounces = 225 g
10 ounces = 285 g
12 ounces = 360 g
16 ounces = 1 pound = 450 g

DIMENSIONS

$^1/_{16}$ inch = 2 mm
$^1/_8$ inch = 3 mm
$^1/_4$ inch = 6 mm
$^1/_2$ inch = 1.5 cm
$^3/_4$ inch = 2 cm
1 inch = 2.5 cm

OVEN TEMPERATURES

250°F = 120°C
275°F = 140°C
300°F = 150°C
325°F = 160°C
350°F = 180°C
375°F = 190°C
400°F = 200°C
425°F = 220°C
450°F = 230°C

BAKING PAN SIZES

Utensil	Size in Inches/Quarts	Metric Volume	Size in Centimeters
Baking or Cake Pan (square or rectangular)	8×8×2	2 L	20×20×5
	9×9×2	2.5 L	23×23×5
	12×8×2	3 L	30×20×5
	13×9×2	3.5 L	33×23×5
Loaf Pan	8×4×3	1.5 L	20×10×7
	9×5×3	2 L	23×13×7
Round Layer Cake Pan	8×1½	1.2 L	20×4
	9×1½	1.5 L	23×4
Pie Plate	8×1¼	750 mL	20×3
	9×1¼	1 L	23×3
Baking Dish or Casserole	1 quart	1 L	—
	1½ quarts	1.5 L	—
	2 quarts	2 L	—